ADOPT-A-BOOK
CHRISTMAS 2016

*Happy Reading!*

# DESTINATION: MARS

## SEYMOUR SIMON

## Updated Edition

**HARPER**
*An Imprint of HarperCollinsPublishers*

*To Liz Nealon, my wife and helpmate*

PHOTO CREDITS
Page 4: © NASA, ESA, and A. Dyer; page 7: © Detlev van Ravenswaay; page 9:
© Percival Lowell; page 11: © Malin Space Science Systems/NASA; page 12: © JPL/
NASA/STScI; page 14–15: © Greg Shirah, SVS; page 16: © NASA/JPL-Caltech/Univ.
of Arizona; page 17: © G. Neukum (FU Berlin) et al., DLR, ESA; page 19: © HiRISE,
MRO, LPL (U. Arizona), NASA; page 20: © NASA/JPL-Caltech/GSFC/Univ. of Arizona;
page 21: © NASA/JPL-Caltech/University of Arizona; page 22: © NASA/JPL-Caltech;
page 25: © NASA/JPL-Caltech/MSSS; page 26: © NASA/JPL-Caltech/MSSS; page 28:
© NASA; page 30–31: © NASA/JPL-Caltech/MSSS.

ISBN 978-0-06-234497-7 (trade bdg.) — ISBN 978-0-06-234504-2 (pbk.)

16  17  18  19  20     SCP     10  9  8  7  6  5  4  3  2  1

❖

Revised edition, 2016

## Author's Note

From a young age, I was interested in animals, space, my surroundings—all the natural sciences. When I was a teenager, I became the president of a nationwide junior astronomy club with a thousand members. After college, I became a classroom teacher for nearly twenty-five years while also writing articles and books for children on science and nature even before I became a full-time writer. My experience as a teacher gives me the ability to understand how to reach my young readers and get them interested in the world around us.

I've written more than 300 books, and I've thought a lot about different ways to encourage interest in the natural world, as well as how to show the joys of nonfiction. When I write, I use comparisons to help explain unfamiliar ideas, complex concepts, and impossibly large numbers. I try to engage your senses and imagination to set the scene and to make science fun. For example, in *Penguins*, I emphasize the playful nature of these creatures on the very first page by mentioning how penguins excel at swimming and diving. I use strong verbs to enhance understanding. I make use of descriptive detail and ask questions that anticipate what you may be thinking (sometimes right at the start of the book).

Many of my books are photo-essays, which use extraordinary photographs to amplify and expand the text, creating different and engaging ways of exploring nonfiction. You'll also find a glossary, an index, and website and research recommendations in most of my books, which make them ideal for enhancing your reading and learning experience. As William Blake wrote in his poem, I want my readers "to see a world in a grain of sand, / And a heaven in a wild flower, / Hold infinity in the palm of your hand, / And eternity in an hour."

*Seymour Simon*

Mars looks like one of the brightest stars in the night sky. But Mars is not a star; it is a planet. Mars appears so bright because it is closer to Earth than any other planet except Venus.

Mars is sometimes called the Red Planet because iron oxide (rust) in the soil makes it shine with a reddish or orange color. Two thousand years ago, the red color reminded the Romans of blood and war. So they named the planet Mars, after their god of war.

Mars is the fourth planet from the sun, after Mercury, Venus, and our own planet, Earth. Mars is more than 140 million miles from the sun—50 million miles farther away from the sun than Earth. It is also a smaller planet than Earth, 4,218 miles across. If Earth were hollow, seven planets the size of Mars could fit inside.

Earth and Mars travel around the sun in paths called orbits. Earth takes one year—365 days—to orbit the sun. But Mars is farther away and takes longer to orbit the sun. A Martian year is 687 Earth days, almost twice as long as a year on Earth. A Martian day is only about half an hour longer than a day on Earth.

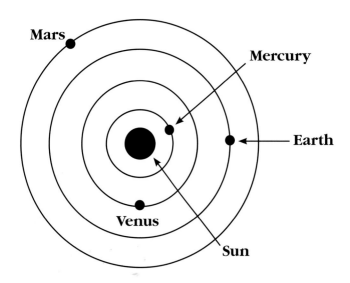

About 150 years ago, an Italian astronomer named Giovanni Schiaparelli studied Mars through a **telescope**. He imagined he saw many straight, dark lines on the surface of the planet. He called them *canali*, the Italian word for "channels," but some people thought he meant "canals."

People heard about the "canals" on Mars. Since they knew that canals are waterways dug by people, they decided that intelligent Martians must have made the canals. Some astronomers drew maps of Mars showing canals crisscrossing the planet.

People began to imagine all kinds of things living on Mars. In 1898, H. G. Wells's book *The War of the Worlds* described tentacled, bug-eyed Martians trying to conquer Earth. Forty years later, a radio play by Orson Welles described Martians invading New Jersey. Thousands of people, believing that the story was real, fled their homes in terror. Since then, there have been many science fiction books, movies, and television programs about invaders from Mars. However, none of the spacecraft scientists sent to Mars have found any canals, or any life at all on the planet.

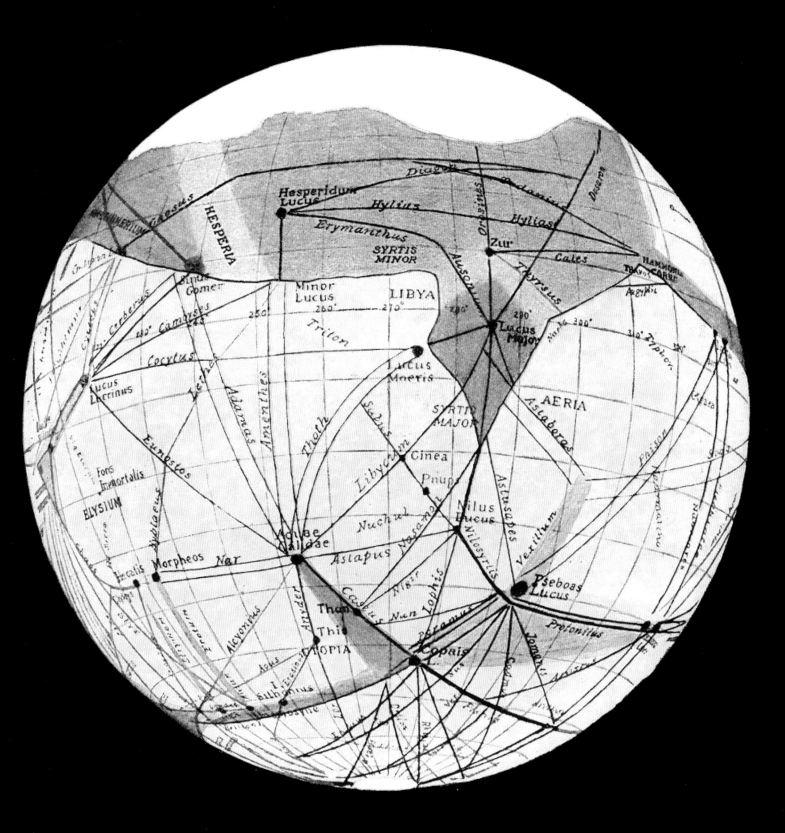

Mars has cooled down, but it was once very hot inside, just like Earth was in the past and still is. Molten rock, called lava, erupted out on the surface of Mars, building huge volcanic peaks.

This is Olympus Mons, the largest known volcano on any planet of the solar system. The Mars global surveyor spacecraft reached Mars in September 1997 and took the photo during one of its orbits around the planet that year.

Olympus Mons rises fifteen miles into the air. This is almost three times as high as Mount Everest, the highest mountain on Earth. The steep base of the volcano would cover the entire state of Missouri. The collapsed center is fifty miles across. Olympus Mons is one of four giant volcanoes in a group just north of the Martian equator.

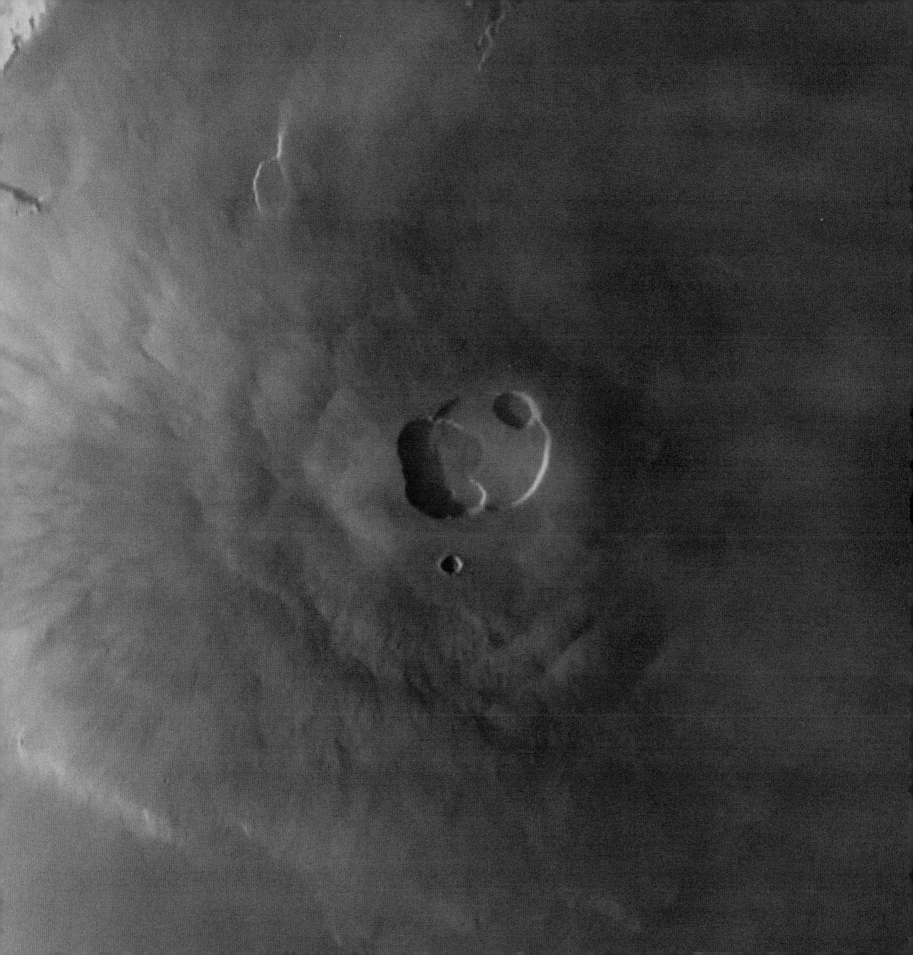

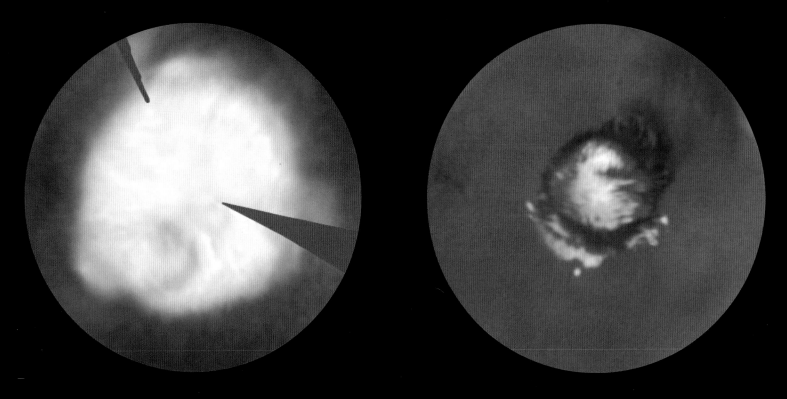

**Winter**

**Summer**

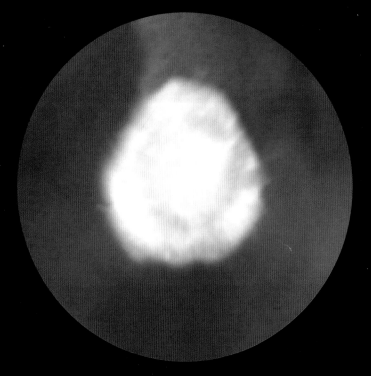

**Spring**

NASA's Hubble Space Telescope (HST) took these images of the north polar ice cap over the course of a Martian year. They show the seasonal changes that take place in the size of the ice cap from the Martian winter (upper left) to spring (lower) to summer (upper right). Other color changes shown in the photographs are the result of dust storms that hide or reveal darker materials on the surface.

The north polar ice cap is composed mostly of water ice, just like Earth's polar ice caps. It has an average thickness of about three thousand feet and covers an area one and a half times the size of Texas. The Martian polar cap has much less ice than Earth's ice caps—they have only 4 percent of the amount in the Antarctic ice sheet, for instance.

An **instrument** called MOLA (Mars Orbiter Laser Altimeter) aboard the Mars global surveyor sent laser pulses toward the planet and measured the time it takes for them to bounce back. Scientists used these measurements to make this three-dimensional photograph and a map of Mars's North Pole in 1998.

The Martian ice cap has canyons that plunge as much as three thousand feet beneath the surface. The canyons are formed by winds cutting through the ice and by the **evaporation** of ice into the **atmosphere**.

Scientists believe that an **ancient** ocean with ten times the amount of water in the ice cap once existed on Mars. They think that the remaining water runs along the surface in the Martian summer and the rest is found in the north polar ice cap, below the surface, as well as in the much smaller south polar cap, or else it has been lost into space.

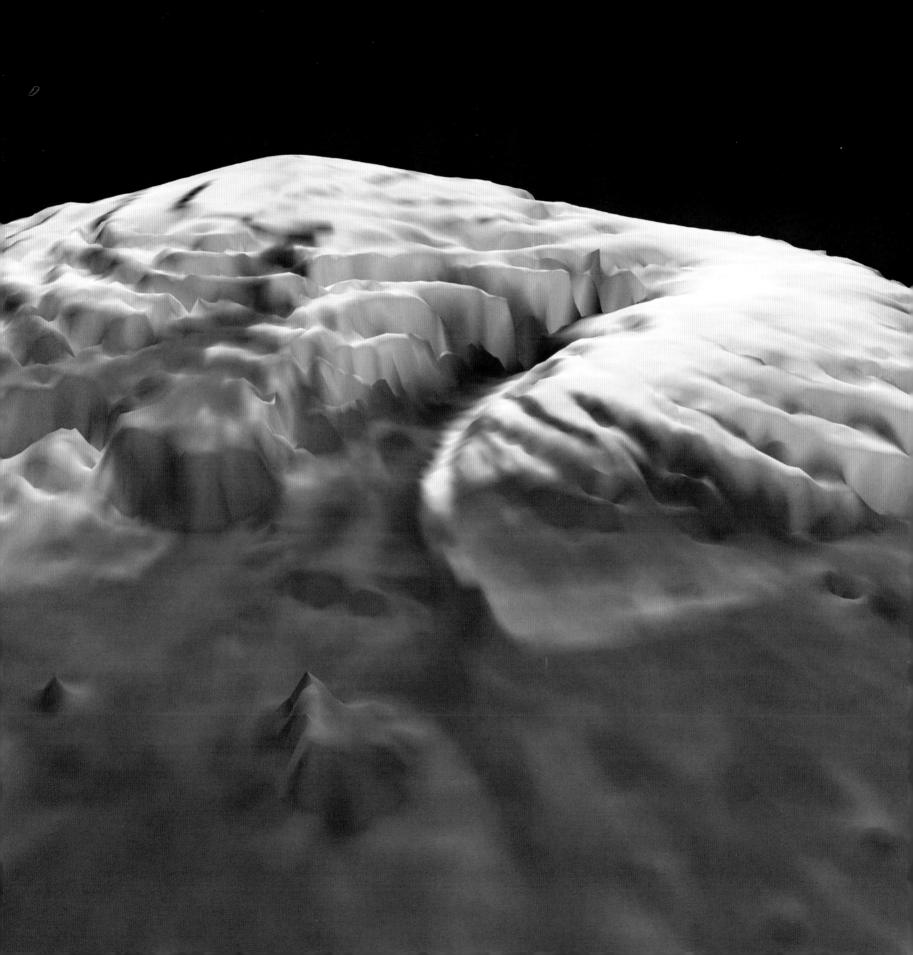

In September 2015, NASA scientists made an important announcement about streams of water flowing across the ancient sands of Mars. They said that seasonal dark streaks seen here on the hillside of a Martian mountain are signs of flowing water that appear every year on Mars. The water is very salty, but it gives the possibility of life. Scientists have not yet discovered life on Mars, but the presence of water supports the idea that life might have existed in the past on the Red Planet.

Europe's Mars Express satellite took this image of a small section of Valles Marineris in 2006. It shows a close-up view of the valleys and ridges on the sides of the canyon. The image is only about forty miles across, but the entire canyon is four times as deep as Arizona's Grand Canyon. If it were on Earth, the canyon would stretch across the United States, from New York to Los Angeles.

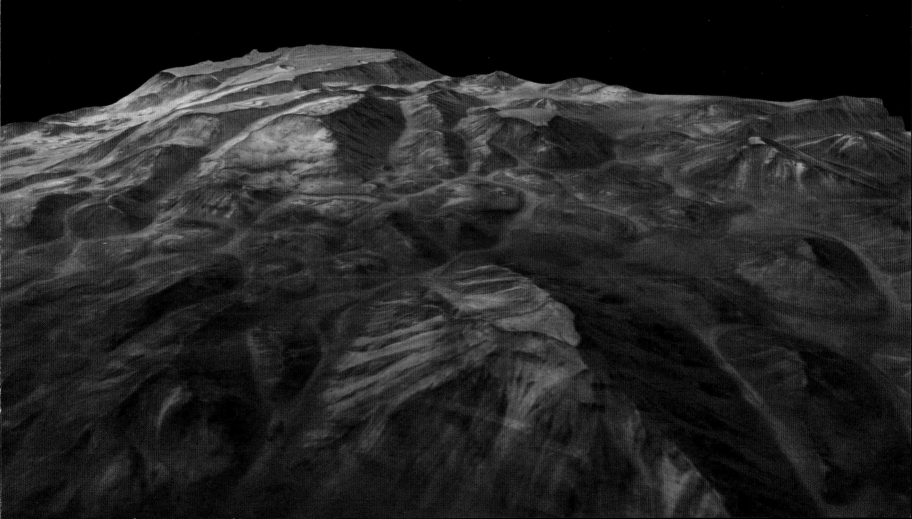

Mars has two small moons, Phobos and Deimos. They are named after the two sons of Ares, the Greek god of war. Phobos [FO-bos] is the larger of the two moons and nearer to Mars. Phobos is about seventeen miles long and twelve miles wide. It races around Mars in only seven and one-half hours, at a distance of about three thousand miles from the planet. If you were an observer on Mars, Phobos would look several times brighter than a very bright star does from Earth. The close-up photo of Phobos shows a giant impact crater named Stickney and a surface **pockmarked** by thousands of **meteorite** impacts.

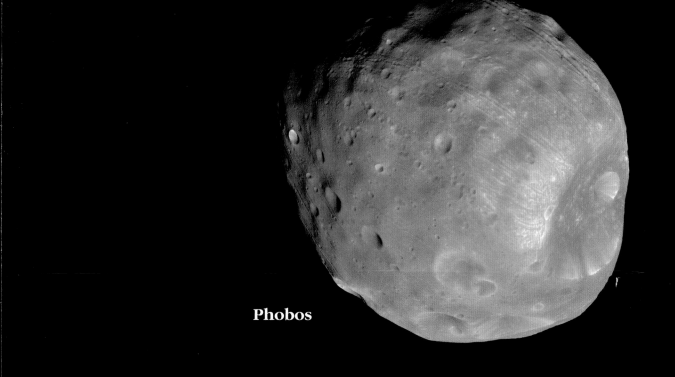

**Phobos**

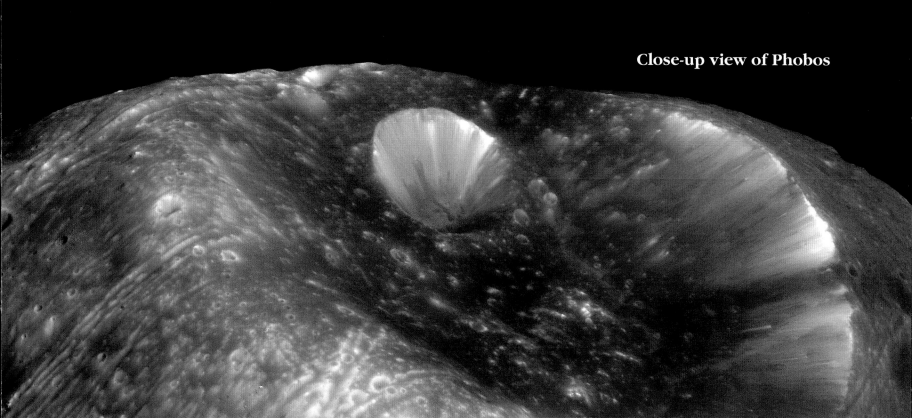

**Close-up view of Phobos**

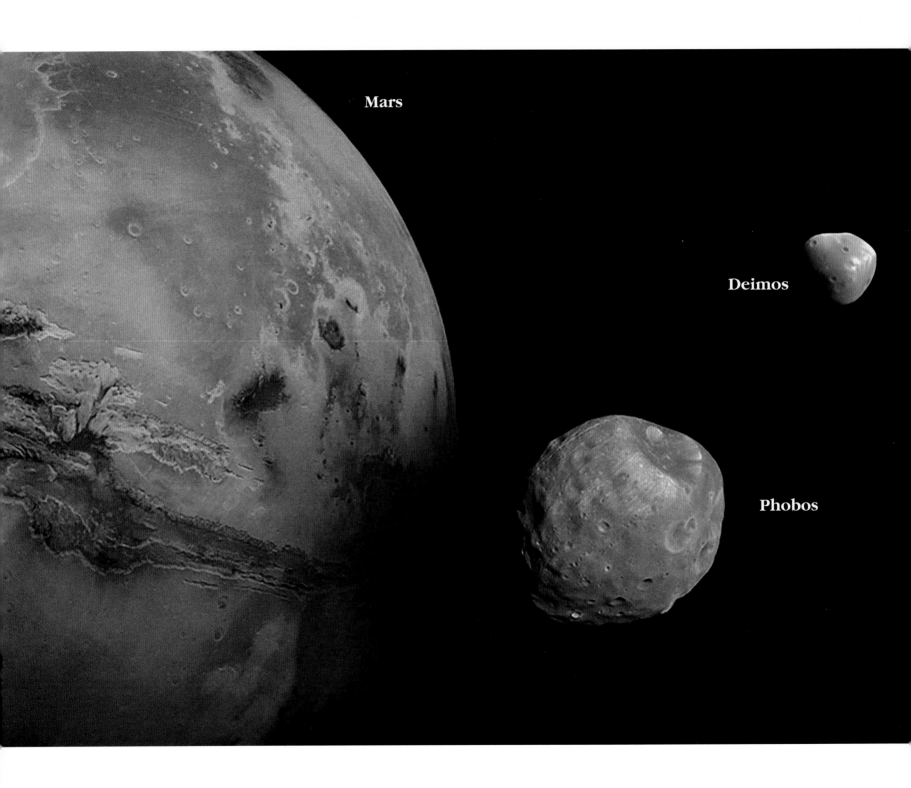

Mars

Deimos

Phobos

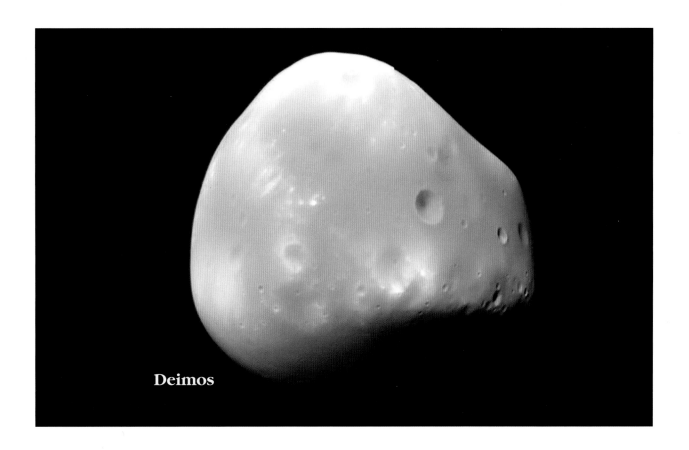

Deimos

Deimos [DIE-mos] is slightly smaller than Phobos, about nine miles long by seven miles wide. Deimos takes a bit longer than thirty hours to orbit Mars and is about 12,500 miles away from the planet. From the surface of Mars, Deimos would look as bright as the planet Venus does from Earth.

Is there life on Mars? Did the planet ever have even small living things called microbes? Scientists are determined to find out. In November 2011, the Mars Science Laboratory sent a spaceship to Mars carrying a Martian rover named *Curiosity.*

The *Curiosity* rover carries the biggest and most advanced instruments ever sent to the surface of Mars. It is able to sample soil scooped from the ground and drilled from rocks. It tests the chemicals in the samples and takes pictures of the Martian landscape. The rover's onboard **laboratory** is trying to find what Mars was like in the past and whether the chemicals needed for life are present on Mars.

The mission reached Mars on August 6, 2012. The spacecraft descended on a parachute. During the final seconds before landing, the ship lowered the *Curiosity* rover on a line to the surface, like a giant sky crane. On Mars, *Curiosity* can travel several hundred feet (more than one hundred meters) per day. It uses its camera and a computer to steer around large rocks. It is powered by electricity from a **radioactive** element that has lasted for more than ten years and will likely last many years more.

The *Curiosity* rover used its own camera at the end of a robotic arm in 2014 to take dozens of photographs that were combined into this "selfie" image. It shows *Curiosity* drilling into a sandstone rock called "Windjana."

Scientists are looking in the soil and rocks on the Martian surface for what are called organic **molecules**. These molecules are the building blocks of all known forms of life back on Earth. They are made mostly from carbon, **hydrogen**, and **oxygen** atoms. But just finding organic molecules on Mars is not enough to prove that there is life now or that it once existed on the planet. Sometimes organic molecules can be made by **chemical reactions** that don't involve life.

Mars probably cannot support life as it exists now. But could the Red Planet have liquid water and a climate that supported life billions of years ago?

The *Curiosity* rover has found that there are sometimes flowing streams of water on Mars, including the rocky outcrop shown here. It has been named "Hottah" after Hottah Lake in Canada. It may look like just a broken sidewalk, but it actually is made of small pieces of rock cemented together by water. Scientists call this kind of rock a **sedimentary conglomerate**. They think that the bedrock of this stream was cracked in the past by impacts made from meteorites.

The key evidence that these rocks were formed in an ancient stream comes from the size and rounded shape of the gravel around the bedrock. The rounded shape shows that they were tumbled by flowing water. The grains are too large to have been moved by the wind.

In the future, there are many missions to Mars on the drawing board. Some are so strange that they sound like science fiction stories rather than straight science.

Exploring Mars "Down Under": Even if we send more rovers to Mars, you can never judge a planet by just its cover. The desertlike surface of the planet may hide the presence of water during the colder months. It may be that some water comes to the surface when it melts during warmer months and the rest of the water is stored belowground in a layer of frost and deeper below that in a liquid lake.

Exploring Mars by air: Scientists hope to fly a Mars airplane or launch a balloon on Mars sometime in the next ten years. They are designing an airplane that can **navigate** without a human pilot. The plane would be able to get better images of the surface and cover more of Mars than a land-based rover. Because the atmosphere is so thin, the airplane would need very big wings and a fast takeoff. Balloons on Mars can stay up longer but are harder to control and would mostly drift with the winds.

his full-circle view is toward the south of Mars at the middle
of the photo, with the north at both ends. It shows the *Curiosity*
rover at the "Rocknest" site. The **panoramic** view in full resolution
contains 1.3 billion pixels and combines nine hundred photos

taken by *Curiosity*. The view of Mars is much clearer and more detailed than any TV picture you have ever seen. We have already learned so much about the planet that someone reading this now may be the first person to set foot on the surface of Mars.

# GLOSSARY

**Ancient**—very old; having existed for a long time.

**Atmosphere**—the blanket of gases that surround Earth or another planet or moon.

**Chemical reaction**—a change in which one or more elements or compounds are changed into one or more different substances. For example, hydrogen and oxygen combine to form water.

**Conglomerate**—a rock made of smaller pieces of rocks or minerals cemented together within a matrix of finer grained materials.

**Evaporation**—the change from a liquid to a gas.

**Hydrogen**—a colorless, highly flammable gas; the lightest of all gases, it is the most abundant element in the universe.

**Instrument**—an electric or mechanical tool or device.

**Laboratory**—a room or building that is used for doing scientific research or experiments.

**Meteorite**—an object from space made of rock and/or metal that hits the surface of a planet, such as Earth, or a moon of a planet.

**Molecule**—a group of two or more atoms linked together by sharing electrons in a chemical bond.

**Navigate**—to manage and control the path of a spaceship, airplane, or other vehicle on its course.

**Oxygen**—an invisible, odorless, and tasteless gas in the atmosphere that is necessary for life.

**Panoramic**—a wide view or picture of a large area.

**Pockmarked**—naturally formed scars or holes in the surface formed by the heavy impact of an object into the surface.

**Radioactive**—a natural or artificial substance that emits radiation.

**Sedimentary**—a kind of rock formed from other rocks naturally deposited in one place.

**Telescope**—an instrument in which an arrangement of lenses and/or other devices is designed to make distant objects appear nearer.

# INDEX

**Bold** type indicates illustrations.

**READ MORE ABOUT IT**

**Seymour Simon's website**
**www.seymoursimon.com**

**National Aeronautics and Space Administration**
**www.nasa.gov**

**Jet Propulsion Laboratory**
**www.jpl.nasa.gov**

**Smithsonian Institution**
**www.si.edu**